Survival Log

NAME

ADDRESS

E-MAIL ADDRESS

WEBSITE

PHONE   **FAX**

EMERGENCY CONTACT PERSON

PHONE   **FAX**

DATE

CONDITIONS

WEATHER ....

TERRAIN ....

SHELTER

SHELTER CONSTRUCTED ☐

TYPE OF SHELTER ....
....
....

CLOTHING/COVERINGS ☐   SUNPROOF ☐

WATERPROOF ☐   FIRE STARTED ☐

ANIMAL PROOF ☐

FOOD INVENTORY

RATIONS ☐	WATER ☐	FISHING ☐
	HUNTING ☐	FORAGING ☐

JOURNEY

DISTANCE COVERED	TRAIL MARKED USED	LANDMARKS SIGHTED	ANIMAL PRINTS

MAP SKETCH

LAT: LONG:

PARTY MEMBER	STATUS	INJURIES	TREATMENT

DATE

CONDITIONS

WEATHER ....

TERRAIN ....

SHELTER

SHELTER CONSTRUCTED ☐

TYPE OF SHELTER ....
....
....

CLOTHING/COVERINGS ☐   **SUNPROOF** ☐

WATERPROOF ☐   **FIRE STARTED** ☐

ANIMAL PROOF ☐

FOOD INVENTORY

RATIONS ☐

....
....
....
....
....

WATER ☐

HUNTING ☐

....
....
....

FISHING ☐

....
....

FORAGING ☐

....
....

JOURNEY

DISTANCE COVERED	TRAIL MARKED USED	LANDMARKS SIGHTED	ANIMAL PRINTS

MAP SKETCH

LAT: **LONG:**

PARTY MEMBER	STATUS	INJURIES	TREATMENT

CONDITIONS

WEATHER ....

TERRAIN ....

SHELTER

SHELTER CONSTRUCTED ☐

TYPE OF SHELTER ....
....
....

CLOTHING/COVERINGS ☐   **SUNPROOF** ☐

WATERPROOF ☐   **FIRE STARTED** ☐

ANIMAL PROOF ☐

FOOD INVENTORY

RATIONS ☐
....
....
....
....
....

WATER ☐

HUNTING ☐
....
....
....
....

FISHING ☐
....
....

FORAGING ☐
....
....

JOURNEY

DISTANCE COVERED	TRAIL MARKED USED	LANDMARKS SIGHTED	ANIMAL PRINTS
....	....	....	....
....	....	....	....
....	....	....	....
....	....	....	....
....	....	....	....
....	....	....	....

MAP SKETCH

LAT: **LONG:**

PARTY MEMBER	STATUS	INJURIES	TREATMENT

DATE

CONDITIONS

WEATHER ....

TERRAIN ....

SHELTER

SHELTER CONSTRUCTED ☐

TYPE OF SHELTER ....
....
....

CLOTHING/COVERINGS ☐   **SUNPROOF** ☐

WATERPROOF ☐   **FIRE STARTED** ☐

ANIMAL PROOF ☐

FOOD INVENTORY

RATIONS ☐
....
....
....
....
....

WATER ☐

HUNTING ☐
....
....
....

FISHING ☐
....
....

FORAGING ☐
....
....

JOURNEY

DISTANCE COVERED	TRAIL MARKED USED	LANDMARKS SIGHTED	ANIMAL PRINTS
....	....	....	....
....	....	....	....
....	....	....	....
....	....	....	....
....	....	....	....
....	....	....	....

MAP SKETCH

LAT: **LONG:**

PARTY MEMBER	STATUS	INJURIES	TREATMENT

CONDITIONS

WEATHER ....

TERRAIN ....

SHELTER

SHELTER CONSTRUCTED ☐

TYPE OF SHELTER ....
....
....

CLOTHING/COVERINGS ☐ **SUNPROOF** ☐

WATERPROOF ☐ **FIRE STARTED** ☐

ANIMAL PROOF ☐

FOOD INVENTORY

RATIONS ☐
....
....
....
....
....

WATER ☐

HUNTING ☐
....
....
....
....

FISHING ☐
....
....

FORAGING ☐
....
....

JOURNEY

DISTANCE COVERED	TRAIL MARKED USED	LANDMARKS SIGHTED	ANIMAL PRINTS

MAP SKETCH

LAT:　　**LONG:**

PARTY MEMBER	STATUS	INJURIES	TREATMENT

DATE

CONDITIONS

WEATHER ....

TERRAIN ....

SHELTER

SHELTER CONSTRUCTED ☐

TYPE OF SHELTER ....
....
....

CLOTHING/COVERINGS ☐ **SUNPROOF** ☐

WATERPROOF ☐ **FIRE STARTED** ☐

ANIMAL PROOF ☐

FOOD INVENTORY

RATIONS ☐

....
....
....
....
....

WATER ☐

HUNTING ☐

....
....
....
....

FISHING ☐

....
....

FORAGING ☐

....
....

JOURNEY

DISTANCE COVERED	TRAIL MARKED USED	LANDMARKS SIGHTED	ANIMAL PRINTS
....	....	....	....
....	....	....	....
....	....	....	....
....	....	....	....
....	....	....	....
....	....	....	....

MAP SKETCH

LAT: **LONG:**

PARTY MEMBER	STATUS	INJURIES	TREATMENT

CONDITIONS

WEATHER ....

TERRAIN ....

SHELTER

SHELTER CONSTRUCTED ☐

TYPE OF SHELTER ....
....
....

CLOTHING/COVERINGS ☐ **SUNPROOF** ☐

WATERPROOF ☐ **FIRE STARTED** ☐

ANIMAL PROOF ☐

FOOD INVENTORY

RATIONS ☐
....
....
....
....
....

WATER ☐

HUNTING ☐
....
....
....
....

FISHING ☐
....
....

FORAGING ☐
....
....

JOURNEY

DISTANCE COVERED	TRAIL MARKED USED	LANDMARKS SIGHTED	ANIMAL PRINTS
....	....	....	....
....	....	....	....
....	....	....	....
....	....	....	....
....	....	....	....
....	....	....	....

MAP SKETCH

LAT: **LONG:**

PARTY MEMBER	STATUS	INJURIES	TREATMENT

CONDITIONS

WEATHER ....

TERRAIN ....

SHELTER

SHELTER CONSTRUCTED ☐

TYPE OF SHELTER ....
....
....

CLOTHING/COVERINGS ☐   **SUNPROOF** ☐

WATERPROOF ☐   **FIRE STARTED** ☐

ANIMAL PROOF ☐

FOOD INVENTORY

RATIONS ☐
....
....
....
....
....

WATER ☐

HUNTING ☐
....
....
....
....

FISHING ☐
....
....

FORAGING ☐
....
....

JOURNEY

DISTANCE COVERED	TRAIL MARKED USED	LANDMARKS SIGHTED	ANIMAL PRINTS
....	....	....	....
....	....	....	....
....	....	....	....
....	....	....	....
....	....	....	....
....	....	....	....

MAP SKETCH

LAT: **LONG:**

PARTY MEMBER	STATUS	INJURIES	TREATMENT

CONDITIONS

WEATHER ....

TERRAIN ....

SHELTER

SHELTER CONSTRUCTED ☐

TYPE OF SHELTER ....
....
....

CLOTHING/COVERINGS ☐

WATERPROOF ☐

ANIMAL PROOF ☐

SUNPROOF ☐

FIRE STARTED ☐

FOOD INVENTORY

RATIONS ☐

WATER ☐

HUNTING ☐

FISHING ☐

FORAGING ☐

JOURNEY

DISTANCE COVERED	TRAIL MARKED USED	LANDMARKS SIGHTED	ANIMAL PRINTS

MAP SKETCH

LAT: **LONG:**

PARTY MEMBER	STATUS	INJURIES	TREATMENT

DATE

CONDITIONS

WEATHER ....

TERRAIN ....

SHELTER

SHELTER CONSTRUCTED ☐

TYPE OF SHELTER ....
....
....

CLOTHING/COVERINGS ☐   SUNPROOF ☐

WATERPROOF ☐   FIRE STARTED ☐

ANIMAL PROOF ☐

FOOD INVENTORY

RATIONS ☐
....
....
....
....
....

WATER ☐

HUNTING ☐
....
....
....
....

FISHING ☐
....
....

FORAGING ☐
....
....

JOURNEY

DISTANCE COVERED	TRAIL MARKED USED	LANDMARKS SIGHTED	ANIMAL PRINTS
....	....	....	....
....	....	....	....
....	....	....	....
....	....	....	....
....	....	....	....
....	....	....	....

MAP SKETCH

LAT: LONG:

PARTY MEMBER	STATUS	INJURIES	TREATMENT

CONDITIONS

WEATHER ....

TERRAIN ....

SHELTER

SHELTER CONSTRUCTED ☐

TYPE OF SHELTER ....
....
....

CLOTHING/COVERINGS ☐   **SUNPROOF** ☐

WATERPROOF ☐   **FIRE STARTED** ☐

ANIMAL PROOF ☐

FOOD INVENTORY

RATIONS ☐
....
....
....
....

WATER ☐

HUNTING ☐
....
....
....
....

FISHING ☐
....
....

FORAGING ☐
....
....

JOURNEY

DISTANCE COVERED	TRAIL MARKED USED	LANDMARKS SIGHTED	ANIMAL PRINTS
....	....	....	....
....	....	....	....
....	....	....	....
....	....	....	....
....	....	....	....
....	....	....	....

MAP SKETCH

LAT: **LONG:**

PARTY MEMBER	STATUS	INJURIES	TREATMENT

DATE

CONDITIONS

WEATHER ....

TERRAIN ....

SHELTER

SHELTER CONSTRUCTED ☐

TYPE OF SHELTER ....
....
....

CLOTHING/COVERINGS ☐

WATERPROOF ☐

ANIMAL PROOF ☐

SUNPROOF ☐

FIRE STARTED ☐

FOOD INVENTORY

RATIONS ☐
....
....
....
....
....

WATER ☐

HUNTING ☐
....
....
....
....

FISHING ☐
....
....

FORAGING ☐
....
....

JOURNEY

DISTANCE COVERED	TRAIL MARKED USED	LANDMARKS SIGHTED	ANIMAL PRINTS
....	....	....	....
....	....	....	....
....	....	....	....
....	....	....	....
....	....	....	....
....	....	....	....

MAP SKETCH

LAT: **LONG:**

PARTY MEMBER	STATUS	INJURIES	TREATMENT

CONDITIONS

WEATHER ....

TERRAIN ....

SHELTER

SHELTER CONSTRUCTED ☐

TYPE OF SHELTER ....
....
....

CLOTHING/COVERINGS ☐   **SUNPROOF** ☐

WATERPROOF ☐   **FIRE STARTED** ☐

ANIMAL PROOF ☐

FOOD INVENTORY

RATIONS ☐	WATER ☐	FISHING ☐
	HUNTING ☐	
		FORAGING ☐

JOURNEY

DISTANCE COVERED	TRAIL MARKED USED	LANDMARKS SIGHTED	ANIMAL PRINTS

MAP SKETCH

LAT: **LONG:**

PARTY MEMBER	STATUS	INJURIES	TREATMENT

DATE

CONDITIONS

WEATHER ....

TERRAIN ....

SHELTER

SHELTER CONSTRUCTED ☐

TYPE OF SHELTER ....

....

....

CLOTHING/COVERINGS ☐ **SUNPROOF** ☐

WATERPROOF ☐ **FIRE STARTED** ☐

ANIMAL PROOF ☐

FOOD INVENTORY

RATIONS ☐

....

....

....

....

....

WATER ☐

HUNTING ☐

....

....

....

FISHING ☐

....

....

FORAGING ☐

....

....

JOURNEY

DISTANCE COVERED	TRAIL MARKED USED	LANDMARKS SIGHTED	ANIMAL PRINTS
....	....	....	....
....	....	....	....
....	....	....	....
....	....	....	....
....	....	....	....
....	....	....	....

MAP SKETCH

LAT: **LONG:**

PARTY MEMBER	STATUS	INJURIES	TREATMENT

CONDITIONS

WEATHER ....

TERRAIN ....

SHELTER

SHELTER CONSTRUCTED ☐

TYPE OF SHELTER ....
....
....

CLOTHING/COVERINGS ☐   **SUNPROOF** ☐

WATERPROOF ☐   **FIRE STARTED** ☐

ANIMAL PROOF ☐

FOOD INVENTORY

RATIONS ☐
....
....
....
....
....

WATER ☐

HUNTING ☐
....
....
....
....

FISHING ☐
....
....

FORAGING ☐
....
....

JOURNEY

DISTANCE COVERED	TRAIL MARKED USED	LANDMARKS SIGHTED	ANIMAL PRINTS
....	....	....	....
....	....	....	....
....	....	....	....
....	....	....	....
....	....	....	....
....	....	....	....

MAP SKETCH

LAT: **LONG:**

PARTY MEMBER	STATUS	INJURIES	TREATMENT

CONDITIONS

WEATHER ....

TERRAIN ....

SHELTER

SHELTER CONSTRUCTED ☐

TYPE OF SHELTER ················

··

··

CLOTHING/COVERINGS ☐ SUNPROOF ☐

WATERPROOF ☐ FIRE STARTED ☐

ANIMAL PROOF ☐

FOOD INVENTORY

RATIONS ☐

···

···

···

···

···

WATER ☐

HUNTING ☐

···

···

···

···

FISHING ☐

···

···

FORAGING ☐

···

···

JOURNEY

DISTANCE COVERED	TRAIL MARKED USED	LANDMARKS SIGHTED	ANIMAL PRINTS
················	················	················	················
················	················	················	················
················	················	················	················
················	················	················	················
················	················	················	················
················	················	················	················

MAP SKETCH

LAT: LONG:

PARTY MEMBER	STATUS	INJURIES	TREATMENT

DATE

CONDITIONS

WEATHER ....

TERRAIN ....

SHELTER

SHELTER CONSTRUCTED ☐

TYPE OF SHELTER ....
....
....

CLOTHING/COVERINGS ☐ **SUNPROOF** ☐

WATERPROOF ☐ **FIRE STARTED** ☐

ANIMAL PROOF ☐

FOOD INVENTORY

RATIONS ☐
....
....
....
....
....

WATER ☐

HUNTING ☐
....
....
....
....

FISHING ☐
....
....

FORAGING ☐
....
....

JOURNEY

DISTANCE COVERED	TRAIL MARKED USED	LANDMARKS SIGHTED	ANIMAL PRINTS

MAP SKETCH

LAT: **LONG:**

PARTY MEMBER	STATUS	INJURIES	TREATMENT

CONDITIONS

WEATHER ....

TERRAIN ....

SHELTER

SHELTER CONSTRUCTED ☐

TYPE OF SHELTER ....

....

....

CLOTHING/COVERINGS ☐   **SUNPROOF** ☐

WATERPROOF ☐   **FIRE STARTED** ☐

ANIMAL PROOF ☐

FOOD INVENTORY

RATIONS ☐   **WATER** ☐   **FISHING** ☐

....   **HUNTING** ☐   ....

....

....   **FORAGING** ☐

....

....

JOURNEY

DISTANCE COVERED	TRAIL MARKED USED	LANDMARKS SIGHTED	ANIMAL PRINTS

MAP SKETCH

LAT: **LONG:**

PARTY MEMBER	STATUS	INJURIES	TREATMENT

CONDITIONS

WEATHER ....

TERRAIN ....

SHELTER

SHELTER CONSTRUCTED ☐

TYPE OF SHELTER ....
....
....

CLOTHING/COVERINGS ☐   **SUNPROOF** ☐

WATERPROOF ☐   **FIRE STARTED** ☐

ANIMAL PROOF ☐

FOOD INVENTORY

RATIONS ☐
....
....
....
....
....

WATER ☐

HUNTING ☐
....
....
....
....

FISHING ☐
....
....

FORAGING ☐
....
....

JOURNEY

DISTANCE COVERED	TRAIL MARKED USED	LANDMARKS SIGHTED	ANIMAL PRINTS

MAP SKETCH

LAT: **LONG:**

PARTY MEMBER	STATUS	INJURIES	TREATMENT

CONDITIONS

WEATHER ....

TERRAIN ....

SHELTER

SHELTER CONSTRUCTED ☐

TYPE OF SHELTER ....
....
....

CLOTHING/COVERINGS ☐   SUNPROOF ☐

WATERPROOF ☐   FIRE STARTED ☐

ANIMAL PROOF ☐

FOOD INVENTORY

RATIONS ☐
....
....
....
....
....

WATER ☐

HUNTING ☐
....
....
....
....

FISHING ☐
....
....

FORAGING ☐
....
....

JOURNEY

DISTANCE COVERED	TRAIL MARKED USED	LANDMARKS SIGHTED	ANIMAL PRINTS

MAP SKETCH

LAT: LONG:

PARTY MEMBER	STATUS	INJURIES	TREATMENT

DATE

CONDITIONS

WEATHER ....

TERRAIN ....

SHELTER

SHELTER CONSTRUCTED ☐

TYPE OF SHELTER ....

....

....

CLOTHING/COVERINGS ☐   **SUNPROOF** ☐

WATERPROOF ☐   **FIRE STARTED** ☐

ANIMAL PROOF ☐

FOOD INVENTORY

RATIONS ☐	WATER ☐	FISHING ☐
	HUNTING ☐	FORAGING ☐

JOURNEY

DISTANCE COVERED	TRAIL MARKED USED	LANDMARKS SIGHTED	ANIMAL PRINTS

MAP SKETCH

LAT: **LONG:**

PARTY MEMBER	STATUS	INJURIES	TREATMENT

DATE

CONDITIONS

WEATHER ....

TERRAIN ....

SHELTER

SHELTER CONSTRUCTED ☐

TYPE OF SHELTER ....

....

....

CLOTHING/COVERINGS ☐   **SUNPROOF** ☐

WATERPROOF ☐   **FIRE STARTED** ☐

ANIMAL PROOF ☐

FOOD INVENTORY

RATIONS ☐

....

....

....

....

....

WATER ☐

HUNTING ☐

....

....

....

....

FISHING ☐

....

....

FORAGING ☐

....

....

JOURNEY

DISTANCE COVERED	TRAIL MARKED USED	LANDMARKS SIGHTED	ANIMAL PRINTS
....	....	....	....
....	....	....	....
....	....	....	....
....	....	....	....
....	....	....	....
....	....	....	....

MAP SKETCH

LAT: **LONG:**

PARTY MEMBER	STATUS	INJURIES	TREATMENT

CONDITIONS

WEATHER ....

TERRAIN ....

SHELTER

SHELTER CONSTRUCTED ☐

TYPE OF SHELTER ....
....
....

CLOTHING/COVERINGS ☐   **SUNPROOF** ☐

WATERPROOF ☐   **FIRE STARTED** ☐

ANIMAL PROOF ☐

FOOD INVENTORY

RATIONS ☐
....
....
....
....

WATER ☐

HUNTING ☐
....
....
....
....

FISHING ☐
....
....

FORAGING ☐
....
....

JOURNEY

DISTANCE COVERED	TRAIL MARKED USED	LANDMARKS SIGHTED	ANIMAL PRINTS

MAP SKETCH

LAT: **LONG:**

PARTY MEMBER	STATUS	INJURIES	TREATMENT

DATE

CONDITIONS

WEATHER ....

TERRAIN ....

SHELTER

SHELTER CONSTRUCTED ☐

TYPE OF SHELTER ....

....

....

CLOTHING/COVERINGS ☐   **SUNPROOF** ☐

WATERPROOF ☐   **FIRE STARTED** ☐

ANIMAL PROOF ☐

FOOD INVENTORY

RATIONS ☐   **WATER** ☐   **FISHING** ☐

HUNTING ☐

FORAGING ☐

JOURNEY

DISTANCE COVERED	TRAIL MARKED USED	LANDMARKS SIGHTED	ANIMAL PRINTS

MAP SKETCH

LAT: **LONG:**

PARTY MEMBER	STATUS	INJURIES	TREATMENT

DATE

CONDITIONS

WEATHER ....

TERRAIN ....

SHELTER

SHELTER CONSTRUCTED ☐

TYPE OF SHELTER ....

....

....

CLOTHING/COVERINGS ☐   **SUNPROOF** ☐

WATERPROOF ☐   **FIRE STARTED** ☐

ANIMAL PROOF ☐

FOOD INVENTORY

RATIONS ☐

....

....

....

....

WATER ☐

HUNTING ☐

....

....

....

....

FISHING ☐

....

....

FORAGING ☐

....

....

JOURNEY

DISTANCE COVERED	TRAIL MARKED USED	LANDMARKS SIGHTED	ANIMAL PRINTS
....	....	....	....
....	....	....	....
....	....	....	....
....	....	....	....
....	....	....	....
....	....	....	....

MAP SKETCH

LAT: **LONG:**

PARTY MEMBER	STATUS	INJURIES	TREATMENT

DATE

CONDITIONS

WEATHER ....

TERRAIN ....

SHELTER

SHELTER CONSTRUCTED ☐   CLOTHING/COVERINGS ☐   SUNPROOF ☐

TYPE OF SHELTER ....   WATERPROOF ☐   FIRE STARTED ☐

....   ANIMAL PROOF ☐

....

FOOD INVENTORY

RATIONS ☐	WATER ☐	FISHING ☐
....	HUNTING ☐	....
....	....	....
....	....	FORAGING ☐
....	....	....
....	....	....

JOURNEY

DISTANCE COVERED	TRAIL MARKED USED	LANDMARKS SIGHTED	ANIMAL PRINTS
....	....	....	....
....	....	....	....
....	....	....	....
....	....	....	....
....	....	....	....
....	....	....	....

MAP SKETCH

LAT: LONG:

PARTY MEMBER	STATUS	INJURIES	TREATMENT

DATE

CONDITIONS

WEATHER ....

TERRAIN ....

SHELTER

SHELTER CONSTRUCTED ☐

TYPE OF SHELTER ....

....

....

CLOTHING/COVERINGS ☐ **SUNPROOF** ☐

WATERPROOF ☐ **FIRE STARTED** ☐

ANIMAL PROOF ☐

FOOD INVENTORY

RATIONS ☐

....

....

....

....

....

WATER ☐

HUNTING ☐

....

....

....

....

....

FISHING ☐

....

....

FORAGING ☐

....

....

JOURNEY

DISTANCE COVERED	TRAIL MARKED USED	LANDMARKS SIGHTED	ANIMAL PRINTS
....	....	....	....
....	....	....	....
....	....	....	....
....	....	....	....
....	....	....	....
....	....	....	....

MAP SKETCH

LAT: **LONG:**

PARTY MEMBER	STATUS	INJURIES	TREATMENT

CONDITIONS

WEATHER ....

TERRAIN ....

SHELTER

SHELTER CONSTRUCTED ☐

TYPE OF SHELTER ....
....
....

CLOTHING/COVERINGS ☐   **SUNPROOF** ☐

WATERPROOF ☐   **FIRE STARTED** ☐

ANIMAL PROOF ☐

FOOD INVENTORY

RATIONS ☐
....
....
....
....
....

WATER ☐

HUNTING ☐
....
....
....
....

FISHING ☐
....
....

FORAGING ☐
....
....

JOURNEY

DISTANCE COVERED	TRAIL MARKED USED	LANDMARKS SIGHTED	ANIMAL PRINTS
....	....	....	....
....	....	....	....
....	....	....	....
....	....	....	....
....	....	....	....
....	....	....	....

MAP SKETCH

LAT: **LONG:**

PARTY MEMBER	STATUS	INJURIES	TREATMENT

CONDITIONS

WEATHER ....

TERRAIN ....

SHELTER

SHELTER CONSTRUCTED ☐

TYPE OF SHELTER ....
....
....

CLOTHING/COVERINGS ☐   **SUNPROOF** ☐

WATERPROOF ☐   **FIRE STARTED** ☐

ANIMAL PROOF ☐

FOOD INVENTORY

RATIONS ☐

....
....
....
....

WATER ☐

HUNTING ☐

....
....
....
....

FISHING ☐

....
....

FORAGING ☐

....
....

JOURNEY

DISTANCE COVERED	TRAIL MARKED USED	LANDMARKS SIGHTED	ANIMAL PRINTS
....	....	....	....
....	....	....	....
....	....	....	....
....	....	....	....
....	....	....	....
....	....	....	....

MAP SKETCH

LAT: **LONG:**

PARTY MEMBER	STATUS	INJURIES	TREATMENT

CONDITIONS

WEATHER ....

TERRAIN ....

SHELTER

SHELTER CONSTRUCTED ☐

TYPE OF SHELTER ....
....
....

CLOTHING/COVERINGS ☐ **SUNPROOF** ☐

WATERPROOF ☐ **FIRE STARTED** ☐

ANIMAL PROOF ☐

FOOD INVENTORY

RATIONS ☐
....
....
....
....
....

WATER ☐

HUNTING ☐
....
....
....
....

FISHING ☐
....
....

FORAGING ☐
....
....

JOURNEY

DISTANCE COVERED	TRAIL MARKED USED	LANDMARKS SIGHTED	ANIMAL PRINTS
....	....	....	....
....	....	....	....
....	....	....	....
....	....	....	....
....	....	....	....
....	....	....	....

MAP SKETCH

LAT: **LONG:**

PARTY MEMBER	STATUS	INJURIES	TREATMENT

DATE

CONDITIONS

WEATHER ....

TERRAIN ....

SHELTER

SHELTER CONSTRUCTED ☐

TYPE OF SHELTER ....
....
....

CLOTHING/COVERINGS ☐   **SUNPROOF** ☐

WATERPROOF ☐   **FIRE STARTED** ☐

ANIMAL PROOF ☐

FOOD INVENTORY

RATIONS ☐	WATER ☐	FISHING ☐
	HUNTING ☐	FORAGING ☐

JOURNEY

DISTANCE COVERED	TRAIL MARKED USED	LANDMARKS SIGHTED	ANIMAL PRINTS

MAP SKETCH

LAT: **LONG:**

PARTY MEMBER	STATUS	INJURIES	TREATMENT

CONDITIONS

WEATHER ....

TERRAIN ....

SHELTER

SHELTER CONSTRUCTED ☐

TYPE OF SHELTER ....

....

....

CLOTHING/COVERINGS ☐   **SUNPROOF** ☐

WATERPROOF ☐   **FIRE STARTED** ☐

ANIMAL PROOF ☐

FOOD INVENTORY

RATIONS ☐

....

....

....

....

....

WATER ☐

HUNTING ☐

....

....

....

....

FISHING ☐

....

....

FORAGING ☐

....

....

JOURNEY

DISTANCE COVERED	TRAIL MARKED USED	LANDMARKS SIGHTED	ANIMAL PRINTS
....	....	....	....
....	....	....	....
....	....	....	....
....	....	....	....
....	....	....	....
....	....	....	....

MAP SKETCH

LAT: **LONG:**

PARTY MEMBER	STATUS	INJURIES	TREATMENT

DATE

CONDITIONS

WEATHER ....

TERRAIN ....

SHELTER

SHELTER CONSTRUCTED ☐	**CLOTHING/COVERINGS** ☐	**SUNPROOF** ☐
TYPE OF SHELTER	**WATERPROOF** ☐	**FIRE STARTED** ☐
....	**ANIMAL PROOF** ☐	
....		

FOOD INVENTORY

RATIONS ☐	**WATER** ☐	**FISHING** ☐
....	**HUNTING** ☐	....
....	....	....
....	....	**FORAGING** ☐
....	....	....
....	....	....

JOURNEY

DISTANCE COVERED	TRAIL MARKED USED	LANDMARKS SIGHTED	ANIMAL PRINTS
....	....	....	....
....	....	....	....
....	....	....	....
....	....	....	....
....	....	....	....
....	....	....	....

MAP SKETCH

LAT: **LONG:**

PARTY MEMBER	STATUS	INJURIES	TREATMENT

DATE

CONDITIONS

WEATHER ....

TERRAIN ....

SHELTER

SHELTER CONSTRUCTED ☐

TYPE OF SHELTER ....

....

....

CLOTHING/COVERINGS ☐

WATERPROOF ☐

ANIMAL PROOF ☐

SUNPROOF ☐

FIRE STARTED ☐

FOOD INVENTORY

RATIONS ☐

WATER ☐

HUNTING ☐

FISHING ☐

FORAGING ☐

JOURNEY

DISTANCE COVERED	TRAIL MARKED USED	LANDMARKS SIGHTED	ANIMAL PRINTS

MAP SKETCH

LAT: **LONG:**

PARTY MEMBER	STATUS	INJURIES	TREATMENT

CONDITIONS

WEATHER ....

TERRAIN ....

SHELTER

SHELTER CONSTRUCTED ☐

TYPE OF SHELTER ....
....
....

CLOTHING/COVERINGS ☐ SUNPROOF ☐

WATERPROOF ☐ FIRE STARTED ☐

ANIMAL PROOF ☐

FOOD INVENTORY

RATIONS ☐
....
....
....
....
....

WATER ☐

HUNTING ☐
....
....
....
....

FISHING ☐
....
....

FORAGING ☐
....
....

JOURNEY

DISTANCE COVERED	TRAIL MARKED USED	LANDMARKS SIGHTED	ANIMAL PRINTS
....	....	....	....
....	....	....	....
....	....	....	....
....	....	....	....
....	....	....	....
....	....	....	....

MAP SKETCH

LAT: LONG:

PARTY MEMBER	STATUS	INJURIES	TREATMENT

DATE

CONDITIONS

WEATHER ....

TERRAIN ....

SHELTER

SHELTER CONSTRUCTED ☐

TYPE OF SHELTER ....
....
....

CLOTHING/COVERINGS ☐   **SUNPROOF** ☐

WATERPROOF ☐   **FIRE STARTED** ☐

ANIMAL PROOF ☐

FOOD INVENTORY

RATIONS ☐
....
....
....
....
....

WATER ☐

HUNTING ☐
....
....
....
....

FISHING ☐
....
....

FORAGING ☐
....
....

JOURNEY

DISTANCE COVERED	TRAIL MARKED USED	LANDMARKS SIGHTED	ANIMAL PRINTS

MAP SKETCH

LAT: **LONG:**

PARTY MEMBER	STATUS	INJURIES	TREATMENT

CONDITIONS

WEATHER ....

TERRAIN ....

SHELTER

SHELTER CONSTRUCTED ☐

TYPE OF SHELTER ....
....
....

CLOTHING/COVERINGS ☐   **SUNPROOF** ☐

WATERPROOF ☐   **FIRE STARTED** ☐

ANIMAL PROOF ☐

FOOD INVENTORY

RATIONS ☐
....
....
....
....
....

WATER ☐

HUNTING ☐
....
....
....

FISHING ☐
....
....

FORAGING ☐
....
....

JOURNEY

DISTANCE COVERED	TRAIL MARKED USED	LANDMARKS SIGHTED	ANIMAL PRINTS
....	....	....	....
....	....	....	....
....	....	....	....
....	....	....	....
....	....	....	....
....	....	....	....

MAP SKETCH

LAT: **LONG:**

PARTY MEMBER	STATUS	INJURIES	TREATMENT

CONDITIONS

WEATHER ....

TERRAIN ....

SHELTER

SHELTER CONSTRUCTED ☐

TYPE OF SHELTER ....
....
....

CLOTHING/COVERINGS ☐ **SUNPROOF** ☐

WATERPROOF ☐ **FIRE STARTED** ☐

ANIMAL PROOF ☐

FOOD INVENTORY

RATIONS ☐

....
....
....
....
....

WATER ☐

HUNTING ☐

....
....
....

FISHING ☐

....
....

FORAGING ☐

....
....

JOURNEY

DISTANCE COVERED	TRAIL MARKED USED	LANDMARKS SIGHTED	ANIMAL PRINTS

MAP SKETCH

LAT: **LONG:**

PARTY MEMBER	STATUS	INJURIES	TREATMENT

CONDITIONS

WEATHER ....

TERRAIN ....

SHELTER

SHELTER CONSTRUCTED ☐

TYPE OF SHELTER ....

....

....

CLOTHING/COVERINGS ☐ **SUNPROOF** ☐

WATERPROOF ☐ **FIRE STARTED** ☐

ANIMAL PROOF ☐

FOOD INVENTORY

RATIONS ☐

....

....

....

....

....

WATER ☐

HUNTING ☐

....

....

....

....

FISHING ☐

....

....

FORAGING ☐

....

....

JOURNEY

DISTANCE COVERED	TRAIL MARKED USED	LANDMARKS SIGHTED	ANIMAL PRINTS
....	....	....	....
....	....	....	....
....	....	....	....
....	....	....	....
....	....	....	....
....	....	....	....

MAP SKETCH

LAT: **LONG:**

PARTY MEMBER	STATUS	INJURIES	TREATMENT

CONDITIONS

WEATHER ....

TERRAIN ....

SHELTER

SHELTER CONSTRUCTED ☐

TYPE OF SHELTER ....
....
....

CLOTHING/COVERINGS ☐

WATERPROOF ☐

ANIMAL PROOF ☐

SUNPROOF ☐

FIRE STARTED ☐

FOOD INVENTORY

RATIONS ☐
....
....
....
....
....

WATER ☐

HUNTING ☐
....
....
....
....

FISHING ☐
....
....

FORAGING ☐
....
....

JOURNEY

DISTANCE COVERED	TRAIL MARKED USED	LANDMARKS SIGHTED	ANIMAL PRINTS
....	....	....	....
....	....	....	....
....	....	....	....
....	....	....	....
....	....	....	....
....	....	....	....

MAP SKETCH

LAT: **LONG:**

PARTY MEMBER	STATUS	INJURIES	TREATMENT

DATE

CONDITIONS

WEATHER ....

TERRAIN ....

SHELTER

SHELTER CONSTRUCTED ☐

TYPE OF SHELTER ....
....
....

CLOTHING/COVERINGS ☐ **SUNPROOF** ☐

WATERPROOF ☐ **FIRE STARTED** ☐

ANIMAL PROOF ☐

FOOD INVENTORY

RATIONS ☐
....
....
....
....
....

WATER ☐

HUNTING ☐
....
....
....
....

FISHING ☐
....
....

FORAGING ☐
....
....

JOURNEY

DISTANCE COVERED	TRAIL MARKED USED	LANDMARKS SIGHTED	ANIMAL PRINTS

MAP SKETCH

LAT: **LONG:**

PARTY MEMBER	STATUS	INJURIES	TREATMENT

CONDITIONS

WEATHER ....

TERRAIN ....

SHELTER

SHELTER CONSTRUCTED ☐

TYPE OF SHELTER ....
....
....

CLOTHING/COVERINGS ☐   **SUNPROOF** ☐

WATERPROOF ☐   **FIRE STARTED** ☐

ANIMAL PROOF ☐

FOOD INVENTORY

RATIONS ☐
....
....
....
....
....

WATER ☐

HUNTING ☐
....
....
....
....

FISHING ☐
....
....

FORAGING ☐
....
....

JOURNEY

DISTANCE COVERED	TRAIL MARKED USED	LANDMARKS SIGHTED	ANIMAL PRINTS
....	....	....	....
....	....	....	....
....	....	....	....
....	....	....	....
....	....	....	....
....	....	....	....

MAP SKETCH

LAT: **LONG:**

PARTY MEMBER	STATUS	INJURIES	TREATMENT

DATE

CONDITIONS

WEATHER ....

TERRAIN ....

SHELTER

SHELTER CONSTRUCTED ☐

TYPE OF SHELTER ....
....
....

CLOTHING/COVERINGS ☐   **SUNPROOF** ☐

WATERPROOF ☐   **FIRE STARTED** ☐

ANIMAL PROOF ☐

FOOD INVENTORY

RATIONS ☐
....
....
....
....

WATER ☐

HUNTING ☐
....
....
....
....

FISHING ☐
....
....

FORAGING ☐
....
....

JOURNEY

DISTANCE COVERED	TRAIL MARKED USED	LANDMARKS SIGHTED	ANIMAL PRINTS
....	....	....	....
....	....	....	....
....	....	....	....
....	....	....	....
....	....	....	....
....	....	....	....

MAP SKETCH

LAT: **LONG:**

PARTY MEMBER	STATUS	INJURIES	TREATMENT

CONDITIONS

WEATHER ....

TERRAIN ....

SHELTER

SHELTER CONSTRUCTED ☐

TYPE OF SHELTER ....
....
....

CLOTHING/COVERINGS ☐

WATERPROOF ☐

ANIMAL PROOF ☐

SUNPROOF ☐

FIRE STARTED ☐

FOOD INVENTORY

RATIONS ☐
....
....
....
....
....

WATER ☐

HUNTING ☐
....
....
....
....

FISHING ☐
....
....

FORAGING ☐
....
....

JOURNEY

DISTANCE COVERED	TRAIL MARKED USED	LANDMARKS SIGHTED	ANIMAL PRINTS
....	....	....	....
....	....	....	....
....	....	....	....
....	....	....	....
....	....	....	....
....	....	....	....

MAP SKETCH

LAT: **LONG:**

PARTY MEMBER	STATUS	INJURIES	TREATMENT

DATE

CONDITIONS

WEATHER ....

TERRAIN ....

SHELTER

SHELTER CONSTRUCTED ☐

TYPE OF SHELTER ....
....
....

CLOTHING/COVERINGS ☐   **SUNPROOF** ☐

WATERPROOF ☐   **FIRE STARTED** ☐

ANIMAL PROOF ☐

FOOD INVENTORY

RATIONS ☐
....
....
....
....
....

WATER ☐

HUNTING ☐
....
....
....
....

FISHING ☐
....
....

FORAGING ☐
....
....

JOURNEY

DISTANCE COVERED	TRAIL MARKED USED	LANDMARKS SIGHTED	ANIMAL PRINTS
....	....	....	....
....	....	....	....
....	....	....	....
....	....	....	....
....	....	....	....
....	....	....	....

MAP SKETCH

LAT: **LONG:**

PARTY MEMBER	STATUS	INJURIES	TREATMENT

CONDITIONS

WEATHER ....

TERRAIN ....

SHELTER

SHELTER CONSTRUCTED ☐

TYPE OF SHELTER ....
....
....

CLOTHING/COVERINGS ☐   **SUNPROOF** ☐

WATERPROOF ☐   **FIRE STARTED** ☐

ANIMAL PROOF ☐

FOOD INVENTORY

RATIONS ☐
....
....
....
....
....

WATER ☐

HUNTING ☐
....
....
....

FISHING ☐
....
....

FORAGING ☐
....
....

JOURNEY

DISTANCE COVERED	TRAIL MARKED USED	LANDMARKS SIGHTED	ANIMAL PRINTS

MAP SKETCH

LAT: **LONG:**

PARTY MEMBER	STATUS	INJURIES	TREATMENT

CONDITIONS

WEATHER ....

TERRAIN ....

SHELTER

SHELTER CONSTRUCTED ☐

TYPE OF SHELTER ....

....

....

CLOTHING/COVERINGS ☐   **SUNPROOF** ☐

WATERPROOF ☐   **FIRE STARTED** ☐

ANIMAL PROOF ☐

FOOD INVENTORY

RATIONS ☐

....

....

....

....

....

WATER ☐

HUNTING ☐

....

....

....

....

FISHING ☐

....

....

FORAGING ☐

....

....

JOURNEY

DISTANCE COVERED	TRAIL MARKED USED	LANDMARKS SIGHTED	ANIMAL PRINTS
....	....	....	....
....	....	....	....
....	....	....	....
....	....	....	....
....	....	....	....
....	....	....	....

MAP SKETCH

LAT: **LONG:**

PARTY MEMBER	STATUS	INJURIES	TREATMENT

DATE

CONDITIONS

WEATHER ....

TERRAIN ....

SHELTER

SHELTER CONSTRUCTED ☐

TYPE OF SHELTER ....
....
....

CLOTHING/COVERINGS ☐   **SUNPROOF** ☐

WATERPROOF ☐   **FIRE STARTED** ☐

ANIMAL PROOF ☐

FOOD INVENTORY

RATIONS ☐
....
....
....
....
....

WATER ☐

HUNTING ☐
....
....
....
....

FISHING ☐
....
....

FORAGING ☐
....
....

JOURNEY

DISTANCE COVERED	TRAIL MARKED USED	LANDMARKS SIGHTED	ANIMAL PRINTS
....	....	....	....
....	....	....	....
....	....	....	....
....	....	....	....
....	....	....	....
....	....	....	....

MAP SKETCH

LAT: **LONG:**

PARTY MEMBER	STATUS	INJURIES	TREATMENT

CONDITIONS

WEATHER ....

TERRAIN ....

SHELTER

SHELTER CONSTRUCTED ☐

TYPE OF SHELTER ....
....
....

CLOTHING/COVERINGS ☐   SUNPROOF ☐

WATERPROOF ☐   FIRE STARTED ☐

ANIMAL PROOF ☐

FOOD INVENTORY

RATIONS ☐

....
....
....
....

WATER ☐

HUNTING ☐

....
....
....
....

FISHING ☐

....
....

FORAGING ☐

....
....

JOURNEY

DISTANCE COVERED	TRAIL MARKED USED	LANDMARKS SIGHTED	ANIMAL PRINTS
....	....	....	....
....	....	....	....
....	....	....	....
....	....	....	....
....	....	....	....
....	....	....	....

MAP SKETCH

LAT: LONG:

PARTY MEMBER	STATUS	INJURIES	TREATMENT

DATE

CONDITIONS

WEATHER ....

TERRAIN ....

SHELTER

SHELTER CONSTRUCTED ☐

TYPE OF SHELTER ....
....
....

CLOTHING/COVERINGS ☐ **SUNPROOF** ☐

WATERPROOF ☐ **FIRE STARTED** ☐

ANIMAL PROOF ☐

FOOD INVENTORY

RATIONS ☐

....
....
....
....
....

WATER ☐

HUNTING ☐

....
....
....
....

FISHING ☐

....
....

FORAGING ☐

....
....

JOURNEY

DISTANCE COVERED	TRAIL MARKED USED	LANDMARKS SIGHTED	ANIMAL PRINTS
....	....	....	....
....	....	....	....
....	....	....	....
....	....	....	....
....	....	....	....
....	....	....	....

MAP SKETCH

LAT: **LONG:**

PARTY MEMBER	STATUS	INJURIES	TREATMENT

DATE

CONDITIONS

WEATHER ....

TERRAIN ....

SHELTER

SHELTER CONSTRUCTED ☐

TYPE OF SHELTER ....

....

....

CLOTHING/COVERINGS ☐ **SUNPROOF** ☐

WATERPROOF ☐ **FIRE STARTED** ☐

ANIMAL PROOF ☐

FOOD INVENTORY

RATIONS ☐

....

....

....

....

....

WATER ☐

HUNTING ☐

....

....

....

....

FISHING ☐

....

....

FORAGING ☐

....

....

JOURNEY

DISTANCE COVERED	TRAIL MARKED USED	LANDMARKS SIGHTED	ANIMAL PRINTS
....	....	....	....
....	....	....	....
....	....	....	....
....	....	....	....
....	....	....	....
....	....	....	....

MAP SKETCH

LAT: **LONG:**

PARTY MEMBER	STATUS	INJURIES	TREATMENT

CONDITIONS

WEATHER ....

TERRAIN ....

SHELTER

SHELTER CONSTRUCTED ☐

TYPE OF SHELTER ....
....
....

CLOTHING/COVERINGS ☐   **SUNPROOF** ☐

WATERPROOF ☐   **FIRE STARTED** ☐

ANIMAL PROOF ☐

FOOD INVENTORY

RATIONS ☐
....
....
....
....
....

WATER ☐

HUNTING ☐
....
....
....
....

FISHING ☐
....
....

FORAGING ☐
....
....

JOURNEY

DISTANCE COVERED	TRAIL MARKED USED	LANDMARKS SIGHTED	ANIMAL PRINTS
....	....	....	....
....	....	....	....
....	....	....	....
....	....	....	....
....	....	....	....
....	....	....	....

MAP SKETCH

LAT: **LONG:**

PARTY MEMBER	STATUS	INJURIES	TREATMENT

CONDITIONS

WEATHER ....

TERRAIN ....

SHELTER

SHELTER CONSTRUCTED ☐

TYPE OF SHELTER ....

....

....

CLOTHING/COVERINGS ☐ **SUNPROOF** ☐

WATERPROOF ☐ **FIRE STARTED** ☐

ANIMAL PROOF ☐

FOOD INVENTORY

RATIONS ☐

....

....

....

....

....

WATER ☐

HUNTING ☐

....

....

....

....

FISHING ☐

....

....

FORAGING ☐

....

....

JOURNEY

DISTANCE COVERED	TRAIL MARKED USED	LANDMARKS SIGHTED	ANIMAL PRINTS
....	....	....	....
....	....	....	....
....	....	....	....
....	....	....	....
....	....	....	....
....	....	....	....

MAP SKETCH

LAT: **LONG:**

PARTY MEMBER	STATUS	INJURIES	TREATMENT

DATE

CONDITIONS

WEATHER ....

TERRAIN ....

SHELTER

SHELTER CONSTRUCTED ☐

TYPE OF SHELTER ....

....

....

CLOTHING/COVERINGS ☐   SUNPROOF ☐

WATERPROOF ☐   FIRE STARTED ☐

ANIMAL PROOF ☐

FOOD INVENTORY

RATIONS ☐

....

....

....

....

....

WATER ☐

HUNTING ☐

....

....

....

....

FISHING ☐

....

....

FORAGING ☐

....

....

....

JOURNEY

DISTANCE COVERED	TRAIL MARKED USED	LANDMARKS SIGHTED	ANIMAL PRINTS
....	....	....	....
....	....	....	....
....	....	....	....
....	....	....	....
....	....	....	....
....	....	....	....

MAP SKETCH

LAT: LONG:

PARTY MEMBER	STATUS	INJURIES	TREATMENT

DATE

CONDITIONS

WEATHER ....

TERRAIN ....

SHELTER

SHELTER CONSTRUCTED ☐

TYPE OF SHELTER ....
....
....

CLOTHING/COVERINGS ☐ **SUNPROOF** ☐

WATERPROOF ☐ **FIRE STARTED** ☐

ANIMAL PROOF ☐

FOOD INVENTORY

RATIONS ☐

....
....
....
....
....

WATER ☐

HUNTING ☐

....
....
....
....

FISHING ☐

....
....

FORAGING ☐

....
....

JOURNEY

DISTANCE COVERED	TRAIL MARKED USED	LANDMARKS SIGHTED	ANIMAL PRINTS

MAP SKETCH

LAT: **LONG:**

PARTY MEMBER	STATUS	INJURIES	TREATMENT

CONDITIONS

WEATHER ....

TERRAIN ....

SHELTER

SHELTER CONSTRUCTED ☐

TYPE OF SHELTER ....
....
....

CLOTHING/COVERINGS ☐   **SUNPROOF** ☐

WATERPROOF ☐   **FIRE STARTED** ☐

ANIMAL PROOF ☐

FOOD INVENTORY

RATIONS ☐
....
....
....
....
....

WATER ☐

HUNTING ☐
....
....
....
....

FISHING ☐
....
....

FORAGING ☐
....
....

JOURNEY

DISTANCE COVERED	TRAIL MARKED USED	LANDMARKS SIGHTED	ANIMAL PRINTS
....	....	....	....
....	....	....	....
....	....	....	....
....	....	....	....
....	....	....	....
....	....	....	....

MAP SKETCH

LAT: **LONG:**

PARTY MEMBER	STATUS	INJURIES	TREATMENT

CONDITIONS

WEATHER ....

TERRAIN ....

SHELTER

SHELTER CONSTRUCTED ☐

TYPE OF SHELTER ....
....
....

CLOTHING/COVERINGS ☐   **SUNPROOF** ☐

WATERPROOF ☐   **FIRE STARTED** ☐

ANIMAL PROOF ☐

FOOD INVENTORY

RATIONS ☐
....
....
....
....
....

WATER ☐

HUNTING ☐
....
....
....
....

FISHING ☐
....
....

FORAGING ☐
....
....
....

JOURNEY

DISTANCE COVERED	TRAIL MARKED USED	LANDMARKS SIGHTED	ANIMAL PRINTS
....	....	....	....
....	....	....	....
....	....	....	....
....	....	....	....
....	....	....	....
....	....	....	....

MAP SKETCH

LAT: **LONG:**

PARTY MEMBER	STATUS	INJURIES	TREATMENT

CONDITIONS

WEATHER ....

TERRAIN ....

SHELTER

SHELTER CONSTRUCTED ☐

TYPE OF SHELTER ....
....
....

CLOTHING/COVERINGS ☐   **SUNPROOF** ☐

WATERPROOF ☐   **FIRE STARTED** ☐

ANIMAL PROOF ☐

FOOD INVENTORY

RATIONS ☐
....
....
....
....
....

WATER ☐

HUNTING ☐
....
....
....
....

FISHING ☐
....
....

FORAGING ☐
....
....

JOURNEY

DISTANCE COVERED	TRAIL MARKED USED	LANDMARKS SIGHTED	ANIMAL PRINTS
....	....	....	....
....	....	....	....
....	....	....	....
....	....	....	....
....	....	....	....
....	....	....	....

MAP SKETCH

LAT: **LONG:**

PARTY MEMBER	STATUS	INJURIES	TREATMENT

DATE

CONDITIONS

WEATHER ....

TERRAIN ....

SHELTER

SHELTER CONSTRUCTED ☐   **CLOTHING/COVERINGS** ☐   **SUNPROOF** ☐

TYPE OF SHELTER ....   **WATERPROOF** ☐   **FIRE STARTED** ☐

....   **ANIMAL PROOF** ☐

....

FOOD INVENTORY

RATIONS ☐	WATER ☐	FISHING ☐
	HUNTING ☐	FORAGING ☐

JOURNEY

DISTANCE COVERED	TRAIL MARKED USED	LANDMARKS SIGHTED	ANIMAL PRINTS

MAP SKETCH

LAT: **LONG:**

PARTY MEMBER	STATUS	INJURIES	TREATMENT

DATE

CONDITIONS

WEATHER ....

TERRAIN ....

SHELTER

SHELTER CONSTRUCTED ☐

TYPE OF SHELTER ....
....
....

CLOTHING/COVERINGS ☐   SUNPROOF ☐

WATERPROOF ☐   FIRE STARTED ☐

ANIMAL PROOF ☐

FOOD INVENTORY

RATIONS ☐
....
....
....
....
....

WATER ☐

HUNTING ☐
....
....
....
....

FISHING ☐
....
....

FORAGING ☐
....
....

JOURNEY

DISTANCE COVERED	TRAIL MARKED USED	LANDMARKS SIGHTED	ANIMAL PRINTS
....	....	....	....
....	....	....	....
....	....	....	....
....	....	....	....
....	....	....	....
....	....	....	....

MAP SKETCH

LAT: LONG:

PARTY MEMBER	STATUS	INJURIES	TREATMENT

DATE

CONDITIONS

WEATHER ....

TERRAIN ....

SHELTER

SHELTER CONSTRUCTED ☐

TYPE OF SHELTER ....
....
....

CLOTHING/COVERINGS ☐ **SUNPROOF** ☐

WATERPROOF ☐ **FIRE STARTED** ☐

ANIMAL PROOF ☐

FOOD INVENTORY

RATIONS ☐

....
....
....
....
....

WATER ☐

HUNTING ☐

....
....
....
....

FISHING ☐

....
....

FORAGING ☐

....
....

JOURNEY

DISTANCE COVERED	TRAIL MARKED USED	LANDMARKS SIGHTED	ANIMAL PRINTS

MAP SKETCH

LAT: **LONG:**

PARTY MEMBER	STATUS	INJURIES	TREATMENT

CONDITIONS

WEATHER ....

TERRAIN ....

SHELTER

SHELTER CONSTRUCTED ☐

TYPE OF SHELTER ....
....
....

CLOTHING/COVERINGS ☐   **SUNPROOF** ☐

WATERPROOF ☐   **FIRE STARTED** ☐

ANIMAL PROOF ☐

FOOD INVENTORY

RATIONS ☐
....
....
....
....
....

WATER ☐

HUNTING ☐
....
....
....
....

FISHING ☐
....
....

FORAGING ☐
....
....

JOURNEY

DISTANCE COVERED	TRAIL MARKED USED	LANDMARKS SIGHTED	ANIMAL PRINTS
....	....	....	....
....	....	....	....
....	....	....	....
....	....	....	....
....	....	....	....
....	....	....	....

MAP SKETCH

LAT: **LONG:**

PARTY MEMBER	STATUS	INJURIES	TREATMENT

DATE

CONDITIONS

WEATHER ....

TERRAIN ....

SHELTER

SHELTER CONSTRUCTED ☐

TYPE OF SHELTER ....

....

....

CLOTHING/COVERINGS ☐   **SUNPROOF** ☐

WATERPROOF ☐   **FIRE STARTED** ☐

ANIMAL PROOF ☐

FOOD INVENTORY

RATIONS ☐

....

....

....

....

....

WATER ☐

HUNTING ☐

....

....

....

....

FISHING ☐

....

....

FORAGING ☐

....

....

JOURNEY

DISTANCE COVERED	TRAIL MARKED USED	LANDMARKS SIGHTED	ANIMAL PRINTS
....	....	....	....
....	....	....	....
....	....	....	....
....	....	....	....
....	....	....	....
....	....	....	....

MAP SKETCH

LAT: **LONG:**

PARTY MEMBER	STATUS	INJURIES	TREATMENT

CONDITIONS

WEATHER ....

TERRAIN ....

SHELTER

SHELTER CONSTRUCTED ☐

TYPE OF SHELTER ....

....

....

CLOTHING/COVERINGS ☐   **SUNPROOF** ☐

WATERPROOF ☐   **FIRE STARTED** ☐

ANIMAL PROOF ☐

FOOD INVENTORY

RATIONS ☐

....

....

....

....

....

WATER ☐

HUNTING ☐

....

....

....

....

FISHING ☐

....

....

FORAGING ☐

....

....

JOURNEY

DISTANCE COVERED	TRAIL MARKED USED	LANDMARKS SIGHTED	ANIMAL PRINTS

MAP SKETCH

LAT: **LONG:**

PARTY MEMBER	STATUS	INJURIES	TREATMENT

CONDITIONS

WEATHER ....

TERRAIN ....

SHELTER

SHELTER CONSTRUCTED ☐

TYPE OF SHELTER ....
....
....

CLOTHING/COVERINGS ☐   **SUNPROOF** ☐

WATERPROOF ☐   **FIRE STARTED** ☐

ANIMAL PROOF ☐

FOOD INVENTORY

RATIONS ☐
....
....
....
....
....

WATER ☐

HUNTING ☐
....
....
....
....

FISHING ☐
....
....

FORAGING ☐
....
....

JOURNEY

DISTANCE COVERED	TRAIL MARKED USED	LANDMARKS SIGHTED	ANIMAL PRINTS

MAP SKETCH

LAT: **LONG:**

PARTY MEMBER	STATUS	INJURIES	TREATMENT

DATE

CONDITIONS

WEATHER ....

TERRAIN ....

SHELTER

SHELTER CONSTRUCTED ☐

TYPE OF SHELTER ....

....

....

CLOTHING/COVERINGS ☐   SUNPROOF ☐

WATERPROOF ☐   FIRE STARTED ☐

ANIMAL PROOF ☐

FOOD INVENTORY

RATIONS ☐

....

....

....

....

....

WATER ☐

HUNTING ☐

....

....

....

....

FISHING ☐

....

....

FORAGING ☐

....

....

JOURNEY

DISTANCE COVERED	TRAIL MARKED USED	LANDMARKS SIGHTED	ANIMAL PRINTS
....	....	....	....
....	....	....	....
....	....	....	....
....	....	....	....
....	....	....	....
....	....	....	....

MAP SKETCH

LAT: LONG:

PARTY MEMBER	STATUS	INJURIES	TREATMENT

DATE

CONDITIONS

WEATHER ....

TERRAIN ....

SHELTER

SHELTER CONSTRUCTED ☐

TYPE OF SHELTER ....

....

....

CLOTHING/COVERINGS ☐ **SUNPROOF** ☐

WATERPROOF ☐ **FIRE STARTED** ☐

ANIMAL PROOF ☐

FOOD INVENTORY

RATIONS ☐

....

....

....

....

....

WATER ☐

HUNTING ☐

....

....

....

....

FISHING ☐

....

....

FORAGING ☐

....

....

JOURNEY

DISTANCE COVERED	TRAIL MARKED USED	LANDMARKS SIGHTED	ANIMAL PRINTS
....	....	....	....
....	....	....	....
....	....	....	....
....	....	....	....
....	....	....	....
....	....	....	....

MAP SKETCH

LAT: **LONG:**

PARTY MEMBER	STATUS	INJURIES	TREATMENT

DATE

CONDITIONS

WEATHER ....

TERRAIN ....

SHELTER

SHELTER CONSTRUCTED ☐

TYPE OF SHELTER ....

....

....

CLOTHING/COVERINGS ☐   **SUNPROOF** ☐

WATERPROOF ☐   **FIRE STARTED** ☐

ANIMAL PROOF ☐

FOOD INVENTORY

RATIONS ☐

....

....

....

....

....

WATER ☐

HUNTING ☐

....

....

....

....

FISHING ☐

....

....

FORAGING ☐

....

....

JOURNEY

DISTANCE COVERED	TRAIL MARKED USED	LANDMARKS SIGHTED	ANIMAL PRINTS
....	....	....	....
....	....	....	....
....	....	....	....
....	....	....	....
....	....	....	....
....	....	....	....

MAP SKETCH

LAT: **LONG:**

PARTY MEMBER	STATUS	INJURIES	TREATMENT

DATE

CONDITIONS

WEATHER ....

TERRAIN ....

SHELTER

SHELTER CONSTRUCTED ☐

TYPE OF SHELTER ....

....

....

CLOTHING/COVERINGS ☐   **SUNPROOF** ☐

WATERPROOF ☐   **FIRE STARTED** ☐

ANIMAL PROOF ☐

FOOD INVENTORY

RATIONS ☐

....

....

....

....

....

WATER ☐

HUNTING ☐

....

....

....

....

FISHING ☐

....

....

FORAGING ☐

....

....

JOURNEY

DISTANCE COVERED	TRAIL MARKED USED	LANDMARKS SIGHTED	ANIMAL PRINTS
....	....	....	....
....	....	....	....
....	....	....	....
....	....	....	....
....	....	....	....
....	....	....	....

MAP SKETCH

LAT: **LONG:**

PARTY MEMBER	STATUS	INJURIES	TREATMENT

DATE

CONDITIONS

WEATHER ....

TERRAIN ....

SHELTER

SHELTER CONSTRUCTED ☐

TYPE OF SHELTER ....
....
....

CLOTHING/COVERINGS ☐   **SUNPROOF** ☐

WATERPROOF ☐   **FIRE STARTED** ☐

ANIMAL PROOF ☐

FOOD INVENTORY

RATIONS ☐
....
....
....
....
....

WATER ☐

HUNTING ☐
....
....
....
....

FISHING ☐
....
....

FORAGING ☐
....
....

JOURNEY

DISTANCE COVERED	TRAIL MARKED USED	LANDMARKS SIGHTED	ANIMAL PRINTS
....	....	....	....
....	....	....	....
....	....	....	....
....	....	....	....
....	....	....	....
....	....	....	....

MAP SKETCH

LAT: **LONG:**

PARTY MEMBER	STATUS	INJURIES	TREATMENT

CONDITIONS

WEATHER ....

TERRAIN ....

SHELTER

SHELTER CONSTRUCTED ☐

TYPE OF SHELTER ....

....

....

CLOTHING/COVERINGS ☐ **SUNPROOF** ☐

WATERPROOF ☐ **FIRE STARTED** ☐

ANIMAL PROOF ☐

FOOD INVENTORY

RATIONS ☐

....

....

....

....

....

WATER ☐

HUNTING ☐

....

....

....

....

FISHING ☐

....

....

FORAGING ☐

....

....

JOURNEY

DISTANCE COVERED	TRAIL MARKED USED	LANDMARKS SIGHTED	ANIMAL PRINTS
....	....	....	....
....	....	....	....
....	....	....	....
....	....	....	....
....	....	....	....
....	....	....	....

MAP SKETCH

LAT: **LONG:**

PARTY MEMBER	STATUS	INJURIES	TREATMENT

DATE

CONDITIONS

WEATHER ....

TERRAIN ....

SHELTER

SHELTER CONSTRUCTED ☐

TYPE OF SHELTER ....
....
....

CLOTHING/COVERINGS ☐   SUNPROOF ☐

WATERPROOF ☐   FIRE STARTED ☐

ANIMAL PROOF ☐

FOOD INVENTORY

RATIONS ☐
....
....
....
....
....

WATER ☐

HUNTING ☐
....
....
....
....

FISHING ☐
....
....

FORAGING ☐
....
....

JOURNEY

DISTANCE COVERED	TRAIL MARKED USED	LANDMARKS SIGHTED	ANIMAL PRINTS
....	....	....	....
....	....	....	....
....	....	....	....
....	....	....	....
....	....	....	....
....	....	....	....

MAP SKETCH

LAT: LONG:

PARTY MEMBER	STATUS	INJURIES	TREATMENT

DATE

CONDITIONS

WEATHER ....

TERRAIN ....

SHELTER

SHELTER CONSTRUCTED ☐

TYPE OF SHELTER ....

....

....

CLOTHING/COVERINGS ☐   **SUNPROOF** ☐

WATERPROOF ☐   **FIRE STARTED** ☐

ANIMAL PROOF ☐

FOOD INVENTORY

RATIONS ☐

....

....

....

....

....

WATER ☐

HUNTING ☐

....

....

....

....

FISHING ☐

....

....

FORAGING ☐

....

....

JOURNEY

DISTANCE COVERED	TRAIL MARKED USED	LANDMARKS SIGHTED	ANIMAL PRINTS
....	....	....	....
....	....	....	....
....	....	....	....
....	....	....	....
....	....	....	....
....	....	....	....

MAP SKETCH

LAT: **LONG:**

PARTY MEMBER	STATUS	INJURIES	TREATMENT

DATE

CONDITIONS

WEATHER ....

TERRAIN ....

SHELTER

SHELTER CONSTRUCTED ☐

TYPE OF SHELTER ....
....
....

CLOTHING/COVERINGS ☐ **SUNPROOF** ☐

WATERPROOF ☐ **FIRE STARTED** ☐

ANIMAL PROOF ☐

FOOD INVENTORY

RATIONS ☐

....
....
....
....
....

WATER ☐

HUNTING ☐

....
....
....
....

FISHING ☐

....
....

FORAGING ☐

....
....

JOURNEY

DISTANCE COVERED	TRAIL MARKED USED	LANDMARKS SIGHTED	ANIMAL PRINTS
....	....	....	....
....	....	....	....
....	....	....	....
....	....	....	....
....	....	....	....
....	....	....	....

MAP SKETCH

LAT: **LONG:**

PARTY MEMBER	STATUS	INJURIES	TREATMENT

CONDITIONS

WEATHER ....

TERRAIN ....

SHELTER

SHELTER CONSTRUCTED ☐

TYPE OF SHELTER ....

....

....

CLOTHING/COVERINGS ☐   **SUNPROOF** ☐

WATERPROOF ☐   **FIRE STARTED** ☐

ANIMAL PROOF ☐

FOOD INVENTORY

RATIONS ☐

....

....

....

....

WATER ☐

HUNTING ☐

....

....

....

....

FISHING ☐

....

....

FORAGING ☐

....

....

JOURNEY

DISTANCE COVERED	TRAIL MARKED USED	LANDMARKS SIGHTED	ANIMAL PRINTS

MAP SKETCH

LAT: **LONG:**

PARTY MEMBER	STATUS	INJURIES	TREATMENT

DATE

CONDITIONS

WEATHER ....

TERRAIN ....

SHELTER

SHELTER CONSTRUCTED ☐

TYPE OF SHELTER ....
....
....

CLOTHING/COVERINGS ☐   SUNPROOF ☐

WATERPROOF ☐   FIRE STARTED ☐

ANIMAL PROOF ☐

FOOD INVENTORY

RATIONS ☐
....
....
....
....
....

WATER ☐

HUNTING ☐
....
....
....
....

FISHING ☐
....
....

FORAGING ☐
....
....

JOURNEY

DISTANCE COVERED	TRAIL MARKED USED	LANDMARKS SIGHTED	ANIMAL PRINTS
....	....	....	....
....	....	....	....
....	....	....	....
....	....	....	....
....	....	....	....
....	....	....	....

MAP SKETCH

LAT: LONG:

PARTY MEMBER	STATUS	INJURIES	TREATMENT

CONDITIONS

WEATHER ....

TERRAIN ....

SHELTER

SHELTER CONSTRUCTED ☐

TYPE OF SHELTER ....
....
....

CLOTHING/COVERINGS ☐

WATERPROOF ☐

ANIMAL PROOF ☐

SUNPROOF ☐

FIRE STARTED ☐

FOOD INVENTORY

RATIONS ☐
....
....
....
....

WATER ☐

HUNTING ☐
....
....
....
....

FISHING ☐
....
....

FORAGING ☐
....
....

JOURNEY

DISTANCE COVERED	TRAIL MARKED USED	LANDMARKS SIGHTED	ANIMAL PRINTS
....	....	....	....
....	....	....	....
....	....	....	....
....	....	....	....
....	....	....	....
....	....	....	....

MAP SKETCH

LAT: **LONG:**

PARTY MEMBER	STATUS	INJURIES	TREATMENT

DATE

CONDITIONS

WEATHER ....

TERRAIN ....

SHELTER

SHELTER CONSTRUCTED ☐

TYPE OF SHELTER ....

....

....

CLOTHING/COVERINGS ☐ **SUNPROOF** ☐

WATERPROOF ☐ **FIRE STARTED** ☐

ANIMAL PROOF ☐

FOOD INVENTORY

RATIONS ☐

....

....

....

....

....

WATER ☐

HUNTING ☐

....

....

....

....

FISHING ☐

....

....

FORAGING ☐

....

....

JOURNEY

DISTANCE COVERED	TRAIL MARKED USED	LANDMARKS SIGHTED	ANIMAL PRINTS

MAP SKETCH

LAT: **LONG:**

PARTY MEMBER	STATUS	INJURIES	TREATMENT

CONDITIONS

WEATHER ....

TERRAIN ....

SHELTER

SHELTER CONSTRUCTED ☐

TYPE OF SHELTER ....

....

....

CLOTHING/COVERINGS ☐   **SUNPROOF** ☐

WATERPROOF ☐   **FIRE STARTED** ☐

ANIMAL PROOF ☐

FOOD INVENTORY

RATIONS ☐

....

....

....

....

....

WATER ☐

HUNTING ☐

....

....

....

FISHING ☐

....

....

FORAGING ☐

....

....

JOURNEY

DISTANCE COVERED	TRAIL MARKED USED	LANDMARKS SIGHTED	ANIMAL PRINTS
....	....	....	....
....	....	....	....
....	....	....	....
....	....	....	....
....	....	....	....
....	....	....	....

MAP SKETCH

LAT: **LONG:**

PARTY MEMBER	STATUS	INJURIES	TREATMENT

CONDITIONS

WEATHER ....

TERRAIN ....

SHELTER

SHELTER CONSTRUCTED ☐

TYPE OF SHELTER ....

....

....

CLOTHING/COVERINGS ☐   **SUNPROOF** ☐

WATERPROOF ☐   **FIRE STARTED** ☐

ANIMAL PROOF ☐

FOOD INVENTORY

RATIONS ☐

....

....

....

....

....

WATER ☐

HUNTING ☐

....

....

....

....

FISHING ☐

....

....

FORAGING ☐

....

....

JOURNEY

DISTANCE COVERED	TRAIL MARKED USED	LANDMARKS SIGHTED	ANIMAL PRINTS
....	....	....	....
....	....	....	....
....	....	....	....
....	....	....	....
....	....	....	....
....	....	....	....

MAP SKETCH

LAT: **LONG:**

PARTY MEMBER	STATUS	INJURIES	TREATMENT

CONDITIONS

WEATHER ....

TERRAIN ....

SHELTER

SHELTER CONSTRUCTED ☐

TYPE OF SHELTER ....
....
....

CLOTHING/COVERINGS ☐   **SUNPROOF** ☐

WATERPROOF ☐   **FIRE STARTED** ☐

ANIMAL PROOF ☐

FOOD INVENTORY

RATIONS ☐
....
....
....
....

WATER ☐

HUNTING ☐
....
....
....
....

FISHING ☐
....
....

FORAGING ☐
....
....

JOURNEY

DISTANCE COVERED	TRAIL MARKED USED	LANDMARKS SIGHTED	ANIMAL PRINTS

MAP SKETCH

LAT: **LONG:**

PARTY MEMBER	STATUS	INJURIES	TREATMENT

DATE

CONDITIONS

WEATHER ....

TERRAIN ....

SHELTER

SHELTER CONSTRUCTED ☐

TYPE OF SHELTER ....

....

....

CLOTHING/COVERINGS ☐   SUNPROOF ☐

WATERPROOF ☐   FIRE STARTED ☐

ANIMAL PROOF ☐

FOOD INVENTORY

RATIONS ☐

....

....

....

....

....

WATER ☐

HUNTING ☐

....

....

....

....

FISHING ☐

....

....

FORAGING ☐

....

....

JOURNEY

DISTANCE COVERED	TRAIL MARKED USED	LANDMARKS SIGHTED	ANIMAL PRINTS
....	....	....	....
....	....	....	....
....	....	....	....
....	....	....	....
....	....	....	....
....	....	....	....

MAP SKETCH

LAT: LONG:

PARTY MEMBER	STATUS	INJURIES	TREATMENT

CONDITIONS

WEATHER ....

TERRAIN ....

SHELTER

SHELTER CONSTRUCTED ☐

TYPE OF SHELTER ....
....
....

CLOTHING/COVERINGS ☐   **SUNPROOF** ☐

WATERPROOF ☐   **FIRE STARTED** ☐

ANIMAL PROOF ☐

FOOD INVENTORY

RATIONS ☐
....
....
....
....
....

WATER ☐

HUNTING ☐
....
....
....
....

FISHING ☐
....
....

FORAGING ☐
....
....

JOURNEY

DISTANCE COVERED	TRAIL MARKED USED	LANDMARKS SIGHTED	ANIMAL PRINTS
....	....	....	....
....	....	....	....
....	....	....	....
....	....	....	....
....	....	....	....
....	....	....	....

MAP SKETCH

LAT: **LONG:**

PARTY MEMBER	STATUS	INJURIES	TREATMENT

CONDITIONS

WEATHER ....

TERRAIN ....

SHELTER

SHELTER CONSTRUCTED ☐

TYPE OF SHELTER ....
....
....

CLOTHING/COVERINGS ☐

WATERPROOF ☐

ANIMAL PROOF ☐

SUNPROOF ☐

FIRE STARTED ☐

FOOD INVENTORY

RATIONS ☐
....
....
....
....
....

WATER ☐

HUNTING ☐
....
....
....
....

FISHING ☐
....
....

FORAGING ☐
....
....

JOURNEY

DISTANCE COVERED	TRAIL MARKED USED	LANDMARKS SIGHTED	ANIMAL PRINTS
....	....	....	....
....	....	....	....
....	....	....	....
....	....	....	....
....	....	....	....
....	....	....	....

MAP SKETCH

LAT: **LONG:**

PARTY MEMBER	STATUS	INJURIES	TREATMENT

DATE

CONDITIONS

WEATHER ....

TERRAIN ....

SHELTER

SHELTER CONSTRUCTED ☐

TYPE OF SHELTER ....
....
....

CLOTHING/COVERINGS ☐   **SUNPROOF** ☐

WATERPROOF ☐   **FIRE STARTED** ☐

ANIMAL PROOF ☐

FOOD INVENTORY

RATIONS ☐
....
....
....
....
....

WATER ☐

HUNTING ☐
....
....
....
....

FISHING ☐
....
....

FORAGING ☐
....
....

JOURNEY

DISTANCE COVERED	TRAIL MARKED USED	LANDMARKS SIGHTED	ANIMAL PRINTS

MAP SKETCH

LAT: **LONG:**

PARTY MEMBER	STATUS	INJURIES	TREATMENT

DATE

CONDITIONS

WEATHER ....

TERRAIN ....

SHELTER

SHELTER CONSTRUCTED ☐

TYPE OF SHELTER ....

....

....

CLOTHING/COVERINGS ☐ **SUNPROOF** ☐

WATERPROOF ☐ **FIRE STARTED** ☐

ANIMAL PROOF ☐

FOOD INVENTORY

RATIONS ☐

....

....

....

....

....

WATER ☐

HUNTING ☐

....

....

....

....

FISHING ☐

....

....

FORAGING ☐

....

....

JOURNEY

DISTANCE COVERED	TRAIL MARKED USED	LANDMARKS SIGHTED	ANIMAL PRINTS
....	....	....	....
....	....	....	....
....	....	....	....
....	....	....	....
....	....	....	....
....	....	....	....

MAP SKETCH

LAT: **LONG:**

PARTY MEMBER	STATUS	INJURIES	TREATMENT

CONDITIONS

WEATHER ....

TERRAIN ....

SHELTER

SHELTER CONSTRUCTED ☐

TYPE OF SHELTER ....
....
....

CLOTHING/COVERINGS ☐   **SUNPROOF** ☐

WATERPROOF ☐   **FIRE STARTED** ☐

ANIMAL PROOF ☐

FOOD INVENTORY

RATIONS ☐
....
....
....
....

WATER ☐

HUNTING ☐
....
....
....
....

FISHING ☐
....
....

FORAGING ☐
....
....

JOURNEY

DISTANCE COVERED	TRAIL MARKED USED	LANDMARKS SIGHTED	ANIMAL PRINTS
....	....	....	....
....	....	....	....
....	....	....	....
....	....	....	....
....	....	....	....
....	....	....	....

MAP SKETCH

LAT: **LONG:**

PARTY MEMBER	STATUS	INJURIES	TREATMENT

DATE ....

CONDITIONS

WEATHER ....

TERRAIN ....

SHELTER

SHELTER CONSTRUCTED ☐

TYPE OF SHELTER ....

....

....

CLOTHING/COVERINGS ☐   SUNPROOF ☐

WATERPROOF ☐   FIRE STARTED ☐

ANIMAL PROOF ☐

FOOD INVENTORY

RATIONS ☐

....

....

....

....

....

WATER ☐

HUNTING ☐

....

....

....

....

FISHING ☐

....

....

FORAGING ☐

....

....

JOURNEY

DISTANCE COVERED	TRAIL MARKED USED	LANDMARKS SIGHTED	ANIMAL PRINTS
....	....	....	....
....	....	....	....
....	....	....	....
....	....	....	....
....	....	....	....
....	....	....	....

MAP SKETCH

LAT: LONG:

PARTY MEMBER	STATUS	INJURIES	TREATMENT

CONDITIONS

WEATHER ....

TERRAIN ....

SHELTER

SHELTER CONSTRUCTED ☐

TYPE OF SHELTER ....
....
....

CLOTHING/COVERINGS ☐   **SUNPROOF** ☐

WATERPROOF ☐   **FIRE STARTED** ☐

ANIMAL PROOF ☐

FOOD INVENTORY

RATIONS ☐
....
....
....
....
....

WATER ☐

HUNTING ☐
....
....
....
....

FISHING ☐
....
....

FORAGING ☐
....
....

JOURNEY

DISTANCE COVERED	TRAIL MARKED USED	LANDMARKS SIGHTED	ANIMAL PRINTS
....	....	....	....
....	....	....	....
....	....	....	....
....	....	....	....
....	....	....	....
....	....	....	....

MAP SKETCH

LAT: **LONG:**

PARTY MEMBER	STATUS	INJURIES	TREATMENT

DATE

CONDITIONS

WEATHER ....

TERRAIN ....

SHELTER

SHELTER CONSTRUCTED ☐

TYPE OF SHELTER ....
....
....

CLOTHING/COVERINGS ☐   SUNPROOF ☐

WATERPROOF ☐   FIRE STARTED ☐

ANIMAL PROOF ☐

FOOD INVENTORY

RATIONS ☐
....
....
....
....
....

WATER ☐

HUNTING ☐
....
....
....
....

FISHING ☐
....
....

FORAGING ☐
....
....

JOURNEY

DISTANCE COVERED	TRAIL MARKED USED	LANDMARKS SIGHTED	ANIMAL PRINTS
....	....	....	....
....	....	....	....
....	....	....	....
....	....	....	....
....	....	....	....
....	....	....	....

MAP SKETCH

LAT: LONG:

PARTY MEMBER	STATUS	INJURIES	TREATMENT

CONDITIONS

WEATHER ....

TERRAIN ....

SHELTER

SHELTER CONSTRUCTED ☐

TYPE OF SHELTER ....

....

....

CLOTHING/COVERINGS ☐ **SUNPROOF** ☐

WATERPROOF ☐ **FIRE STARTED** ☐

ANIMAL PROOF ☐

FOOD INVENTORY

RATIONS ☐

....

....

....

....

....

WATER ☐

HUNTING ☐

....

....

....

....

FISHING ☐

....

....

FORAGING ☐

....

....

JOURNEY

DISTANCE COVERED	TRAIL MARKED USED	LANDMARKS SIGHTED	ANIMAL PRINTS
....	....	....	....
....	....	....	....
....	....	....	....
....	....	....	....
....	....	....	....
....	....	....	....

MAP SKETCH

LAT: **LONG:**

PARTY MEMBER	STATUS	INJURIES	TREATMENT

CONDITIONS

WEATHER ....

TERRAIN ....

SHELTER

SHELTER CONSTRUCTED ☐

TYPE OF SHELTER ....
....
....

CLOTHING/COVERINGS ☐ **SUNPROOF** ☐

WATERPROOF ☐ **FIRE STARTED** ☐

ANIMAL PROOF ☐

FOOD INVENTORY

RATIONS ☐
....
....
....
....
....

WATER ☐

HUNTING ☐
....
....
....
....

FISHING ☐
....
....

FORAGING ☐
....
....

JOURNEY

DISTANCE COVERED	TRAIL MARKED USED	LANDMARKS SIGHTED	ANIMAL PRINTS
....	....	....	....
....	....	....	....
....	....	....	....
....	....	....	....
....	....	....	....
....	....	....	....

MAP SKETCH

LAT: **LONG:**

PARTY MEMBER	STATUS	INJURIES	TREATMENT

DATE

CONDITIONS

WEATHER ....

TERRAIN ....

SHELTER

SHELTER CONSTRUCTED ☐

TYPE OF SHELTER ....
....
....

CLOTHING/COVERINGS ☐   **SUNPROOF** ☐

WATERPROOF ☐   **FIRE STARTED** ☐

ANIMAL PROOF ☐

FOOD INVENTORY

RATIONS ☐   **WATER** ☐   **FISHING** ☐

     HUNTING ☐   **FORAGING** ☐

JOURNEY

DISTANCE COVERED	TRAIL MARKED USED	LANDMARKS SIGHTED	ANIMAL PRINTS

MAP SKETCH

LAT: **LONG:**

PARTY MEMBER	STATUS	INJURIES	TREATMENT

DATE

CONDITIONS

WEATHER ....

TERRAIN ....

SHELTER

SHELTER CONSTRUCTED ☐

TYPE OF SHELTER ....

....

....

CLOTHING/COVERINGS ☐   **SUNPROOF** ☐

WATERPROOF ☐   **FIRE STARTED** ☐

ANIMAL PROOF ☐

FOOD INVENTORY

RATIONS ☐

....

....

....

....

....

WATER ☐

HUNTING ☐

....

....

....

....

FISHING ☐

....

....

FORAGING ☐

....

....

JOURNEY

DISTANCE COVERED	TRAIL MARKED USED	LANDMARKS SIGHTED	ANIMAL PRINTS
....	....	....	....
....	....	....	....
....	....	....	....
....	....	....	....
....	....	....	....
....	....	....	....

MAP SKETCH

LAT: **LONG:**

PARTY MEMBER	STATUS	INJURIES	TREATMENT

CONDITIONS

WEATHER ....

TERRAIN ....

SHELTER

SHELTER CONSTRUCTED ☐

TYPE OF SHELTER ....
....
....

CLOTHING/COVERINGS ☐   **SUNPROOF** ☐

WATERPROOF ☐   **FIRE STARTED** ☐

ANIMAL PROOF ☐

FOOD INVENTORY

RATIONS ☐
....
....
....
....
....

WATER ☐

HUNTING ☐
....
....
....
....

FISHING ☐
....
....

FORAGING ☐
....
....

JOURNEY

DISTANCE COVERED	TRAIL MARKED USED	LANDMARKS SIGHTED	ANIMAL PRINTS
....	....	....	....
....	....	....	....
....	....	....	....
....	....	....	....
....	....	....	....
....	....	....	....

MAP SKETCH

LAT: **LONG:**

PARTY MEMBER	STATUS	INJURIES	TREATMENT

DATE ....

CONDITIONS

WEATHER ....

TERRAIN ....

SHELTER

SHELTER CONSTRUCTED ☐

TYPE OF SHELTER ....
....
....

CLOTHING/COVERINGS ☐ **SUNPROOF** ☐

WATERPROOF ☐ **FIRE STARTED** ☐

ANIMAL PROOF ☐

FOOD INVENTORY

RATIONS ☐
....
....
....
....
....

WATER ☐

HUNTING ☐
....
....
....
....

FISHING ☐
....
....

FORAGING ☐
....
....

JOURNEY

DISTANCE COVERED	TRAIL MARKED USED	LANDMARKS SIGHTED	ANIMAL PRINTS
....	....	....	....
....	....	....	....
....	....	....	....
....	....	....	....
....	....	....	....
....	....	....	....

MAP SKETCH

LAT: **LONG:**

PARTY MEMBER	STATUS	INJURIES	TREATMENT

DATE ________________

CONDITIONS

WEATHER ....

TERRAIN ....

SHELTER

SHELTER CONSTRUCTED ☐

TYPE OF SHELTER ....
....
....

CLOTHING/COVERINGS ☐   **SUNPROOF** ☐

WATERPROOF ☐   **FIRE STARTED** ☐

ANIMAL PROOF ☐

FOOD INVENTORY

RATIONS ☐

....
....
....
....
....

WATER ☐

HUNTING ☐

....
....
....
....

FISHING ☐

....
....

FORAGING ☐

....
....

JOURNEY

DISTANCE COVERED	TRAIL MARKED USED	LANDMARKS SIGHTED	ANIMAL PRINTS

MAP SKETCH

LAT: **LONG:**

PARTY MEMBER	STATUS	INJURIES	TREATMENT

DATE

CONDITIONS

WEATHER ....

TERRAIN ....

SHELTER

SHELTER CONSTRUCTED ☐

TYPE OF SHELTER ....
....
....

CLOTHING/COVERINGS ☐   **SUNPROOF** ☐

WATERPROOF ☐   **FIRE STARTED** ☐

ANIMAL PROOF ☐

FOOD INVENTORY

RATIONS ☐
....
....
....
....
....

WATER ☐

HUNTING ☐
....
....
....
....

FISHING ☐
....
....

FORAGING ☐
....
....

JOURNEY

DISTANCE COVERED	TRAIL MARKED USED	LANDMARKS SIGHTED	ANIMAL PRINTS
....	....	....	....
....	....	....	....
....	....	....	....
....	....	....	....
....	....	....	....
....	....	....	....

MAP SKETCH

LAT: **LONG:**

PARTY MEMBER	STATUS	INJURIES	TREATMENT

CONDITIONS

WEATHER ....

TERRAIN ....

SHELTER

SHELTER CONSTRUCTED ☐

TYPE OF SHELTER ....
....
....

CLOTHING/COVERINGS ☐   **SUNPROOF** ☐

WATERPROOF ☐   **FIRE STARTED** ☐

ANIMAL PROOF ☐

FOOD INVENTORY

RATIONS ☐
....
....
....
....
....

WATER ☐

HUNTING ☐
....
....
....
....

FISHING ☐
....
....

FORAGING ☐
....
....

JOURNEY

DISTANCE COVERED	TRAIL MARKED USED	LANDMARKS SIGHTED	ANIMAL PRINTS

MAP SKETCH

LAT: **LONG:**

PARTY MEMBER	STATUS	INJURIES	TREATMENT

CONDITIONS

WEATHER ....

TERRAIN ....

SHELTER

SHELTER CONSTRUCTED ☐

TYPE OF SHELTER ....

....

....

CLOTHING/COVERINGS ☐   SUNPROOF ☐

WATERPROOF ☐   FIRE STARTED ☐

ANIMAL PROOF ☐

FOOD INVENTORY

RATIONS ☐

....

....

....

....

....

WATER ☐

HUNTING ☐

....

....

....

....

FISHING ☐

....

....

FORAGING ☐

....

....

JOURNEY

DISTANCE COVERED	TRAIL MARKED USED	LANDMARKS SIGHTED	ANIMAL PRINTS
....	....	....	....
....	....	....	....
....	....	....	....
....	....	....	....
....	....	....	....
....	....	....	....

MAP SKETCH

LAT: LONG:

PARTY MEMBER	STATUS	INJURIES	TREATMENT

DATE

CONDITIONS

WEATHER ....

TERRAIN ....

SHELTER

SHELTER CONSTRUCTED ☐

TYPE OF SHELTER ....

....

....

CLOTHING/COVERINGS ☐   SUNPROOF ☐

WATERPROOF ☐   FIRE STARTED ☐

ANIMAL PROOF ☐

FOOD INVENTORY

RATIONS ☐	WATER ☐	FISHING ☐
	HUNTING ☐	
		FORAGING ☐

JOURNEY

DISTANCE COVERED	TRAIL MARKED USED	LANDMARKS SIGHTED	ANIMAL PRINTS

MAP SKETCH

LAT: LONG:

PARTY MEMBER	STATUS	INJURIES	TREATMENT

DATE

CONDITIONS

WEATHER ....

TERRAIN ....

SHELTER

SHELTER CONSTRUCTED ☐

TYPE OF SHELTER ....
....
....

CLOTHING/COVERINGS ☐   SUNPROOF ☐

WATERPROOF ☐   FIRE STARTED ☐

ANIMAL PROOF ☐

FOOD INVENTORY

RATIONS ☐
....
....
....
....
....

WATER ☐

HUNTING ☐
....
....
....
....

FISHING ☐
....
....

FORAGING ☐
....
....

JOURNEY

DISTANCE COVERED	TRAIL MARKED USED	LANDMARKS SIGHTED	ANIMAL PRINTS

MAP SKETCH

LAT: LONG:

PARTY MEMBER	STATUS	INJURIES	TREATMENT

CONDITIONS

WEATHER ....

TERRAIN ....

SHELTER

SHELTER CONSTRUCTED ☐

TYPE OF SHELTER ....
....
....

CLOTHING/COVERINGS ☐   **SUNPROOF** ☐

WATERPROOF ☐   **FIRE STARTED** ☐

ANIMAL PROOF ☐

FOOD INVENTORY

RATIONS ☐	WATER ☐	FISHING ☐
	HUNTING ☐	FORAGING ☐

JOURNEY

DISTANCE COVERED	TRAIL MARKED USED	LANDMARKS SIGHTED	ANIMAL PRINTS

MAP SKETCH

LAT: **LONG:**

PARTY MEMBER	STATUS	INJURIES	TREATMENT

CONDITIONS

WEATHER ....

TERRAIN ....

SHELTER

SHELTER CONSTRUCTED ☐

TYPE OF SHELTER ....
....
....

CLOTHING/COVERINGS ☐   SUNPROOF ☐

WATERPROOF ☐   FIRE STARTED ☐

ANIMAL PROOF ☐

FOOD INVENTORY

RATIONS ☐	WATER ☐	FISHING ☐
	HUNTING ☐	FORAGING ☐

JOURNEY

DISTANCE COVERED	TRAIL MARKED USED	LANDMARKS SIGHTED	ANIMAL PRINTS

MAP SKETCH

LAT: LONG:

PARTY MEMBER	STATUS	INJURIES	TREATMENT

DATE

CONDITIONS

WEATHER ....

TERRAIN ....

SHELTER

SHELTER CONSTRUCTED ☐

TYPE OF SHELTER ....
....
....

CLOTHING/COVERINGS ☐   SUNPROOF ☐

WATERPROOF ☐   FIRE STARTED ☐

ANIMAL PROOF ☐

FOOD INVENTORY

RATIONS ☐

....
....
....
....
....

WATER ☐

HUNTING ☐

....
....
....
....

FISHING ☐

....
....

FORAGING ☐

....
....

JOURNEY

DISTANCE COVERED	TRAIL MARKED USED	LANDMARKS SIGHTED	ANIMAL PRINTS

MAP SKETCH

LAT: LONG:

PARTY MEMBER	STATUS	INJURIES	TREATMENT

DATE

CONDITIONS

WEATHER ....

TERRAIN ....

SHELTER

SHELTER CONSTRUCTED ☐

TYPE OF SHELTER ....

....

....

CLOTHING/COVERINGS ☐   **SUNPROOF** ☐

WATERPROOF ☐   **FIRE STARTED** ☐

ANIMAL PROOF ☐

FOOD INVENTORY

RATIONS ☐

....

....

....

....

....

WATER ☐

HUNTING ☐

....

....

....

FISHING ☐

....

....

FORAGING ☐

....

....

JOURNEY

DISTANCE COVERED	TRAIL MARKED USED	LANDMARKS SIGHTED	ANIMAL PRINTS
....	....	....	....
....	....	....	....
....	....	....	....
....	....	....	....
....	....	....	....
....	....	....	....

MAP SKETCH

LAT: **LONG:**

PARTY MEMBER	STATUS	INJURIES	TREATMENT

DATE

CONDITIONS

WEATHER ....

TERRAIN ....

SHELTER

SHELTER CONSTRUCTED ☐

TYPE OF SHELTER ....

....

....

CLOTHING/COVERINGS ☐   **SUNPROOF** ☐

WATERPROOF ☐   **FIRE STARTED** ☐

ANIMAL PROOF ☐

FOOD INVENTORY

RATIONS ☐   **WATER** ☐   **FISHING** ☐

      HUNTING ☐   **FORAGING** ☐

JOURNEY

DISTANCE COVERED	TRAIL MARKED USED	LANDMARKS SIGHTED	ANIMAL PRINTS

MAP SKETCH

LAT: **LONG:**

PARTY MEMBER	STATUS	INJURIES	TREATMENT

CONDITIONS

WEATHER ....

TERRAIN ....

SHELTER

SHELTER CONSTRUCTED ☐

TYPE OF SHELTER ....

....

....

CLOTHING/COVERINGS ☐   SUNPROOF ☐

WATERPROOF ☐   FIRE STARTED ☐

ANIMAL PROOF ☐

FOOD INVENTORY

RATIONS ☐

....

....

....

....

....

WATER ☐

HUNTING ☐

....

....

....

....

FISHING ☐

....

....

FORAGING ☐

....

....

JOURNEY

DISTANCE COVERED	TRAIL MARKED USED	LANDMARKS SIGHTED	ANIMAL PRINTS
....	....	....	....
....	....	....	....
....	....	....	....
....	....	....	....
....	....	....	....
....	....	....	....

MAP SKETCH

LAT: LONG:

PARTY MEMBER	STATUS	INJURIES	TREATMENT

DATE

CONDITIONS

WEATHER ....

TERRAIN ....

SHELTER

SHELTER CONSTRUCTED ☐

TYPE OF SHELTER ....

....

....

CLOTHING/COVERINGS ☐   SUNPROOF ☐

WATERPROOF ☐   FIRE STARTED ☐

ANIMAL PROOF ☐

FOOD INVENTORY

RATIONS ☐

....

....

....

....

....

WATER ☐

HUNTING ☐

....

....

....

....

FISHING ☐

....

....

FORAGING ☐

....

....

JOURNEY

DISTANCE COVERED	TRAIL MARKED USED	LANDMARKS SIGHTED	ANIMAL PRINTS
....	....	....	....
....	....	....	....
....	....	....	....
....	....	....	....
....	....	....	....
....	....	....	....

MAP SKETCH

LAT: LONG:

PARTY MEMBER	STATUS	INJURIES	TREATMENT

DATE

CONDITIONS

WEATHER ....

TERRAIN ....

SHELTER

SHELTER CONSTRUCTED ☐   CLOTHING/COVERINGS ☐   SUNPROOF ☐

TYPE OF SHELTER ....   WATERPROOF ☐   FIRE STARTED ☐

....   ANIMAL PROOF ☐

....

FOOD INVENTORY

RATIONS ☐	WATER ☐	FISHING ☐
....	HUNTING ☐	....
....	....	....
....	....	FORAGING ☐
....	....	....
....	....	....

JOURNEY

DISTANCE COVERED	TRAIL MARKED USED	LANDMARKS SIGHTED	ANIMAL PRINTS
....	....	....	....
....	....	....	....
....	....	....	....
....	....	....	....
....	....	....	....
....	....	....	....

MAP SKETCH

LAT: LONG:

PARTY MEMBER	STATUS	INJURIES	TREATMENT

DATE

CONDITIONS

WEATHER ....

TERRAIN ....

SHELTER

SHELTER CONSTRUCTED ☐

TYPE OF SHELTER ....
....
....

CLOTHING/COVERINGS ☐ SUNPROOF ☐

WATERPROOF ☐ FIRE STARTED ☐

ANIMAL PROOF ☐

FOOD INVENTORY

RATIONS ☐	WATER ☐	FISHING ☐
....	HUNTING ☐	....
....	....	....
....	....	FORAGING ☐
....	....	....
....	....	....

JOURNEY

DISTANCE COVERED	TRAIL MARKED USED	LANDMARKS SIGHTED	ANIMAL PRINTS
....	....	....	....
....	....	....	....
....	....	....	....
....	....	....	....
....	....	....	....
....	....	....	....

MAP SKETCH

LAT: LONG:

PARTY MEMBER	STATUS	INJURIES	TREATMENT

DATE

CONDITIONS

WEATHER ....

TERRAIN ....

SHELTER

SHELTER CONSTRUCTED ☐

TYPE OF SHELTER ....

....

....

CLOTHING/COVERINGS ☐   SUNPROOF ☐

WATERPROOF ☐   FIRE STARTED ☐

ANIMAL PROOF ☐

FOOD INVENTORY

RATIONS ☐

....

....

....

....

....

WATER ☐

HUNTING ☐

....

....

....

....

FISHING ☐

....

....

FORAGING ☐

....

....

JOURNEY

DISTANCE COVERED	TRAIL MARKED USED	LANDMARKS SIGHTED	ANIMAL PRINTS
....	....	....	....
....	....	....	....
....	....	....	....
....	....	....	....
....	....	....	....
....	....	....	....

MAP SKETCH

LAT: LONG:

PARTY MEMBER	STATUS	INJURIES	TREATMENT

CONDITIONS

WEATHER ....

TERRAIN ....

SHELTER

SHELTER CONSTRUCTED ☐

TYPE OF SHELTER ....
....
....

CLOTHING/COVERINGS ☐ SUNPROOF ☐

WATERPROOF ☐ FIRE STARTED ☐

ANIMAL PROOF ☐

FOOD INVENTORY

RATIONS ☐
....
....
....
....

WATER ☐

HUNTING ☐
....
....
....
....

FISHING ☐
....
....

FORAGING ☐
....
....

JOURNEY

DISTANCE COVERED	TRAIL MARKED USED	LANDMARKS SIGHTED	ANIMAL PRINTS

MAP SKETCH

LAT: LONG:

PARTY MEMBER	STATUS	INJURIES	TREATMENT

DATE

CONDITIONS

WEATHER ....

TERRAIN ....

SHELTER

SHELTER CONSTRUCTED ☐

TYPE OF SHELTER ....
....
....

CLOTHING/COVERINGS ☐   SUNPROOF ☐

WATERPROOF ☐   FIRE STARTED ☐

ANIMAL PROOF ☐

FOOD INVENTORY

RATIONS ☐
....
....
....
....
....

WATER ☐

HUNTING ☐
....
....
....
....

FISHING ☐
....
....

FORAGING ☐
....
....

JOURNEY

DISTANCE COVERED	TRAIL MARKED USED	LANDMARKS SIGHTED	ANIMAL PRINTS

MAP SKETCH

LAT: LONG:

PARTY MEMBER	STATUS	INJURIES	TREATMENT

CONDITIONS

WEATHER ....

TERRAIN ....

SHELTER

SHELTER CONSTRUCTED ☐

TYPE OF SHELTER ....

....

....

CLOTHING/COVERINGS ☐   SUNPROOF ☐

WATERPROOF ☐   FIRE STARTED ☐

ANIMAL PROOF ☐

FOOD INVENTORY

RATIONS ☐

....
....
....
....
....

WATER ☐

HUNTING ☐

....
....
....
....

FISHING ☐

....
....

FORAGING ☐

....
....

JOURNEY

DISTANCE COVERED	TRAIL MARKED USED	LANDMARKS SIGHTED	ANIMAL PRINTS

MAP SKETCH

LAT: LONG:

PARTY MEMBER	STATUS	INJURIES	TREATMENT

DATE

CONDITIONS

WEATHER ....

TERRAIN ....

SHELTER

SHELTER CONSTRUCTED ☐

TYPE OF SHELTER ....

....

....

CLOTHING/COVERINGS ☐ SUNPROOF ☐

WATERPROOF ☐ FIRE STARTED ☐

ANIMAL PROOF ☐

FOOD INVENTORY

RATIONS ☐

....

....

....

....

....

WATER ☐

HUNTING ☐

....

....

....

....

FISHING ☐

....

....

FORAGING ☐

....

....

JOURNEY

DISTANCE COVERED	TRAIL MARKED USED	LANDMARKS SIGHTED	ANIMAL PRINTS
....	....	....	....
....	....	....	....
....	....	....	....
....	....	....	....
....	....	....	....
....	....	....	....

MAP SKETCH

LAT: LONG:

PARTY MEMBER	STATUS	INJURIES	TREATMENT

DATE

CONDITIONS

WEATHER ....

TERRAIN ....

SHELTER

SHELTER CONSTRUCTED ☐

TYPE OF SHELTER ....
....
....

CLOTHING/COVERINGS ☐   **SUNPROOF** ☐

WATERPROOF ☐   **FIRE STARTED** ☐

ANIMAL PROOF ☐

FOOD INVENTORY

RATIONS ☐
....
....
....
....
....

WATER ☐

HUNTING ☐
....
....
....
....

FISHING ☐
....
....

FORAGING ☐
....
....

JOURNEY

DISTANCE COVERED	TRAIL MARKED USED	LANDMARKS SIGHTED	ANIMAL PRINTS
....	....	....	....
....	....	....	....
....	....	....	....
....	....	....	....
....	....	....	....
....	....	....	....

MAP SKETCH

LAT: **LONG:**

PARTY MEMBER	STATUS	INJURIES	TREATMENT

DATE

CONDITIONS

WEATHER ....

TERRAIN ....

SHELTER

SHELTER CONSTRUCTED ☐

TYPE OF SHELTER ....

....

....

CLOTHING/COVERINGS ☐   SUNPROOF ☐

WATERPROOF ☐   FIRE STARTED ☐

ANIMAL PROOF ☐

FOOD INVENTORY

RATIONS ☐

....

....

....

....

....

WATER ☐

HUNTING ☐

....

....

....

....

FISHING ☐

....

....

FORAGING ☐

....

....

JOURNEY

DISTANCE COVERED	TRAIL MARKED USED	LANDMARKS SIGHTED	ANIMAL PRINTS
....	....	....	....
....	....	....	....
....	....	....	....
....	....	....	....
....	....	....	....
....	....	....	....

MAP SKETCH

LAT: LONG:

PARTY MEMBER	STATUS	INJURIES	TREATMENT

CONDITIONS

WEATHER ....

TERRAIN ....

SHELTER

SHELTER CONSTRUCTED ☐

TYPE OF SHELTER ....
....
....

CLOTHING/COVERINGS ☐ **SUNPROOF** ☐

WATERPROOF ☐ **FIRE STARTED** ☐

ANIMAL PROOF ☐

FOOD INVENTORY

RATIONS ☐
....
....
....
....
....

WATER ☐

HUNTING ☐
....
....
....
....

FISHING ☐
....
....

FORAGING ☐
....
....

JOURNEY

DISTANCE COVERED	TRAIL MARKED USED	LANDMARKS SIGHTED	ANIMAL PRINTS

MAP SKETCH

LAT: **LONG:**

PARTY MEMBER	STATUS	INJURIES	TREATMENT